Woodlands

Louise and Richard Spilsbury

Heinemann
LIBRARY

www.heinemann.co.uk/library
Visit our website to find out more information about **Heinemann Library** books.

To order:
☎ Phone 44 (0) 1865 888066
📄 Send a fax to 44 (0) 1865 314091
💻 Visit the Heinemann Bookshop at www.heinemann.co.uk/library to browse our catalogue and order online.

First published in Great Britain by Heinemann Library, Halley Court, Jordan Hill, Oxford OX2 8EJ, part of Harcourt Education.

Heinemann is a registered trademark of Harcourt Education Ltd.

Editorial: Lucy Thunder and Helen Cannons
Design: David Poole and Kamae Design
Picture Research: Hannah Taylor and Liz Savery
Production: Edward Moore

Originated by P. T. Repro Multi-Warna
Printed in China by WKT Company Limited

The paper used to print this book comes from sustainable resources.

ISBN 0 431 12125 7 (hardback)
08 07 06 05 04
10 9 8 7 6 5 4 3 2 1

ISBN 0 431 12132 X (paperback)
09 08 07 06 05
10 9 8 7 6 5 4 3 2 1

British Library Cataloguing in Publication Data
Spilsbury, Louise and Spilsbury, Richard
Woodlands. – (Wild habitats of the British Isles)
577.3'0941
A full catalogue record for this book is available from the British Library.

Acknowledgements
The Publishers would like to thank the following for permission to reproduce photographs: Al Anderson p**18** bottom; Alamy images p**23**; Bruce Coleman/Mark Taylor p**24**; Bruce Coleman/Robert Maier p**17**; FLPA/Ray Bird p**20**; FLPA/Roger Wilmshurst p**5**; John Cleare Mountain Camera p**29**; John Morris/Chiltern Woods Project p**28**; Nature Picture Library/David Noton p**25** bottom; Nature Picture Library/Kevin J Keatley p**13**; Nature Picture Library/Michael W Richards p**6**; Nature Picture Library/Niall Benvie p**27**; Nature Picture Library/Tim Edwards p**15**; NHPA/G J Cambridge p**9**; Ordnance Survey pp**12** left, **18** top, **22** top; Peter Evans pp**7**, **8**, **12** right, **14**, **16**, **25** top; Woodfall Wild Images p**26**; Woodfall Wild Images/Andy Harmer p**21**; Woodfall Wild Images/Jan Halady p**19**; Woodfall Wild Images/John Robinson p**22** bottom; Woodfall Wild Images/Mark Hamblin p**11**

Cover photograph of a bluebell wood, reproduced with permission of Woodfall Wild Images.

The Publishers would like to thank Michael Scott, wildlife consultant and writer, for his assistance in the preparation of this book.

Every effort has been made to contact copyright holders of any material reproduced in this book. Any omissions will be rectified in subsequent printings if notice is given to the Publishers.

Contents

Any words appearing in the text in bold, **like this**,
are explained in the Glossary.

Woodland habitats

Woodlands are areas of land that are covered in trees. Trees are like other plants in that they have leaves, stems and roots, but trees are larger than most other plants. Trees also have tough thick woody stems, called trunks, to support their heavy branches. Different woodlands contain different kinds of trees. The only difference between woodlands and forests is size – forests are just large woodlands, so we will talk about forests in this book, too.

Get this!

Around 8000 years ago 80 per cent of land in the British Isles was covered with trees! Today, only about ten per cent of the land is made up of woodland.

Woodlands in the past

Long ago forests and woodlands covered most of the land in the British Isles. Then, about 8000 years ago, people started to cut down the trees to clear land for farming and building and to use the wood. Even though there are far fewer areas of trees left today, the woodlands that remain are very important **habitats** for many different kinds of plants and animals.

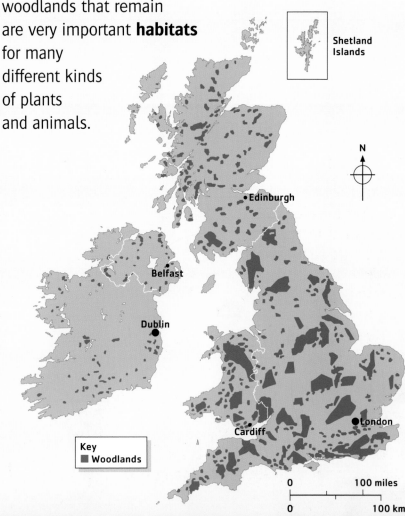

Shetland Islands

N

• Edinburgh

Belfast

Dublin

Cardiff

•London

Key
■ Woodlands

This map shows the main areas of forest and woodland in the British Isles. ➔

| 0 | 100 miles |
| 0 | 100 km |

Woodland habitats

There are many different kinds of habitat within any woodland. Some animals find food and have young among the branches of the woodland canopy – the leafy treetops. Some animals make their home under tree bark or in holes within tree trunks. Some live among the smaller plants growing below the trees. Others live among the **leaf litter**, the rotting piles of leaves that fall from trees and carpet the woodland floor. Below ground, in the soil and among the tree roots, there is yet another habitat teeming with life.

Living together

The organisms (living things) in any woodland live together and rely on each other for survival – they are interdependent. Some woodland **fungi** live on the roots of particular tree **species**. They produce chemicals that break down leaf litter around the roots. The fungi use some of the **nutrients** they release, but some of the spare goes into the tree roots. These nutrients are vital for tree growth. In return, the fungi get sugar from the roots. If you walk through woodland like the one in the picture, you may not notice many of them, but there are thousands of animals living among the trees.

How do woodlands form?

There are many different ways in which trees can grow to form woodlands. Some woodlands in the British Isles are planted by people so they can harvest the trees for wood. Most **plantations** use just a few kinds of quick-growing **conifer** trees such as sitka spruce or Douglas fir.

Wild woodlands

A greater variety of trees grow in wild woodlands. Some **species** such as oak, beech, Scots pine and yew are **native** to the British Isles – they have grown naturally here for thousands of years. Other woodland trees, such as horse chestnut and sycamore, have been **introduced** to the British Isles. This means people brought their seeds from other countries to grow here, either because the trees were useful or they looked attractive. They have survived and in many cases spread naturally by seed because the climate here is similar to the climate of their native country.

Kielder Forest in Northumberland is one of Europe's largest plantations and contains over 150 million trees! ↓

Sitka spruce

Sitka spruce is a conifer that was introduced to the British Isles in 1831. It has stiff, pointed leaves and flaky purple-brown bark. Sitka spruce can grow to over 40 metres tall within 40 years, especially in damper places. Its white wood is used for timber and to make paper.

Growing from seed

Trees reproduce using seeds. If seeds fall on to soil with the right growing conditions – such as sufficient water and space – they may **germinate**. A food store inside the seed provides **energy** for the young tree to grow its first roots and leaves. Once the seedling (young plant) has grown leaves, it makes its own food by **photosynthesis**. Leaves use energy from sunlight to turn carbon dioxide (a gas from the air) and water into sugars. The tree uses the sugar and **nutrients** sucked up through its roots from the soil with water, to grow bigger. The roots also anchor the tree in the ground.

Many seeds do not germinate because the growing conditions are wrong. Often there is too much shade from other trees. Seeds and young trees may also be eaten by **herbivores**.

Get this!

There is less than a one in a million chance of an acorn growing into a mature oak tree.

↑ Trees grow tall woody trunks in woodland as they compete to reach the light. They hold their leaves out on strong branches so they can make as much food as possible.

Broadleaved woodland

Trees such as oak, beech and birch dominate **broadleaved** woodland in the British Isles. These are all trees with wide, soft leaves. The leaves are broad and flat, which gives them a large surface to catch light for **photosynthesis**. Thin pipes called veins stiffen their leaves. The veins carry water and **nutrients** into the leaves from the tree's roots via the trunk. They also carry sugar made by photosynthesis to other parts of the tree where it is used as food.

Tree shapes

Each **species** of broadleaf tree looks different. For example, beech trees have grey, smooth bark whereas sweet chestnut trees have twisted, ridged brown bark. Trees also look different because of where they grow. For example, a tree in the middle of woodland competing for light with other trees is often taller and narrower than one of the same species growing on its own without as much shade.

Dropping off

Most broadleaved trees share an important **adaptation** to life in the British Isles. Britain's climate has warm, wet spring and summer months with a short, cold winter. Large leaves would be damaged by the cold and lose too much water by **evaporation** in the winds of winter.

↑ This mature oak tree is typical of its species, with wide-spreading branches and a rounded shape.

Many broadleaved trees avoid this by getting rid of their leaves all at once in autumn and making new ones in spring. These are known as **deciduous** trees. The new leaves develop during winter inside protective **buds**. In spring, the tiny leaves inside the bud grow and swell until the bud bursts open and the leaves unfold.

Leaf litter

Fallen leaves are rotted down quickly by **fungi** and **bacteria** that live in woodland soil. The fungi we usually see are called mushrooms and toadstools. Most of any fungus is actually a hidden network of cotton-like threads.

Layers of rotting leaves are called **leaf litter**. The nutrients released from leaves produce a rich soil. Many smaller plants grow in the soil if they have enough water and light. Some **germinate** from seeds, but bluebells, wood anemone and ramsons also emerge from underground **bulbs**.

↑ Deciduous leaves, such as these horse chestnut leaves, turn yellow, red and brown as they die and fall to the ground.

Ramsons

There is one woodland flower you can usually smell before you see it. Ramsons are a kind of wild garlic, with a strong smell similar to the garlic we use in cooking. It has long, wide leaves shaped like spearheads and white, star-shaped flowers.

Broadleaved wildlife

Broadleaved woodland provides food, shelter and places to breed for many types of wildlife. Some spend their lives on particular parts of a tree, while others roam over whole woodlands.

Insects and centipedes

Many **insects**, such as butterflies and moths, lay their eggs on leaves. The **larvae** that hatch out of the eggs feed on the leaf surface. Leaf miner larvae have flattened bodies small enough to burrow within leaves. Here they can feed out of sight of **predators**. Some beetle larvae have strong jaws to eat into the hard wood of broadleaved trees beneath the bark, leaving intricate patterns of tunnels.

Ants, ladybirds, spiders and bush crickets are some of the animals that feed on the leaf-eaters. Bush crickets are large green insects with giant back legs they use for leaping around. The female has a sharp, curved egg-laying tube that looks a bit like a stinger. They use eyesight and sensitive **antennae** to find their **prey**.

Centipedes are fast-moving **invertebrates** with 30 legs. They roam through **leaf litter** hunting for woodlice, springtails, slugs and millipedes, which feed on rotting wood and leaf litter. Centipedes kill their prey by injecting them with poison from the tips of their jaws.

There are many different **food webs** in broadleaved woodland in the British Isles. Here is a diagram of a woodland floor food web that starts with leaf litter. ↓

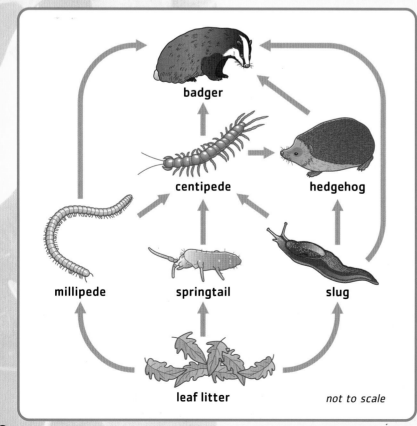

badger

centipede   hedgehog

millipede   springtail   slug

leaf litter   *not to scale*

Birds and mammals

Broadleaved woodlands are full of birds. Some, such as tits, eat the invertebrates on leaves, and some, such as jays, eat the rich supply of nuts. Others, such as tawny owls, hunt smaller birds and **mammals**. Great spotted woodpeckers are black and white. Males have red on their neck and under their tail. They reach beetle larvae beneath bark by drilling through it, using their strong, pointed beak. They drum rapidly on hollow tree trunks to let other great spotted woodpeckers know they are there.

Several mammals, ranging in size from large fallow deer to small shrews, live on the woodland floor. Some, such as badgers and wood mice, make burrows in spaces amongst tree roots where they rest during the day. They feed at night on invertebrates, nuts and seeds. Grey squirrels are active amongst the leafy branches during the day, searching for nuts, berries, bird eggs and chicks to eat.

Treecreepers and nuthatches

Treecreepers are small brown and white birds that creep jerkily up tree trunks, pulling out insects from cracks in the bark using their sharp, curved beak. Nuthatches, like this one, are grey-backed and orange-brown underneath. Unlike treecreepers they often hop down tree trunks in search of insects and seeds. Nuthatches often wedge hard nuts into bark to grip them while they peck them open.

Yarner Wood, England

Yarner Wood is an ancient **broadleaved** oak woodland in Dartmoor, Devon. The oaks at Yarner are descendants of trees that grew there thousands of years ago. Other **native** trees, such as holly, grow amongst the oaks.

Oak life

Yarner Wood is sheltered from bad weather and the air is moist and unpolluted. These conditions are ideal for mosses, smaller **ferns** and **lichen** that grow slowly attached to oaks. Tree lungwort is a shaggy green lichen that fringes many Yarner tree trunks.

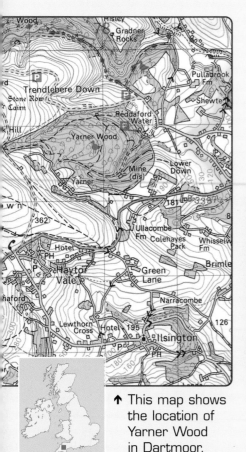

↑ This map shows the location of Yarner Wood in Dartmoor, Devon. Green areas indicate woodlands.

↑ Yarner Wood is part of a National Nature Reserve that also includes heath and river **habitats**.

Life on an oak leaf

Oak leaves are eaten in large quantities by moth **larvae**. Adult green oak moths are small and bright green. They lay their eggs on **buds**. The larvae that hatch eat the soft leaves that emerge. They are **prey** for birds such as wood warblers. Small yellow-green or red discs on the underside of oak leaves are spangle galls. Galls are special growths on plants caused by tiny animals. Each spangle gall is about 3 millimetres across. They grow around the eggs of tiny gall wasps.

Like other broadleaved trees, oak is a flowering plant. Its tiny flowers that appear in spring are **pollinated** by wind. Oak bears large woody fruits called acorns. Acorns are a favourite food of jays and squirrels that live in Yarner Wood.

Visiting birds

Some birds, such as redstarts, nightjars and spotted flycatchers spend only part of the year in Yarner Wood. Spotted flycatchers are small black and white birds that spend winter in West Africa. Some visit Yarner Wood each summer to **breed**. They build nests in hollows in old oak trees and feed their chicks on flying **insects** such as butterflies.

Badgers

Badgers are large **mammals** that are easy to recognize with their black and white striped faces. Many badgers make their homes in Yarner Wood. They rest during the day in setts – tunnels and rooms they dig under trees. They often mark entrance holes to a sett by scratching trees nearby. Badgers may move several kilometres through the woods at night searching for food. They snuffle through **leaf litter**, using their sense of smell to find earthworms, **invertebrates** and fallen nuts and fruit. If you see badger footprints in a woodland like these shown, you might be near a badger sett!

Coniferous woodland

Conifer trees dominate conifer woodlands. Conifers make their seeds in **cones** instead of fruits. Cones are made up of lots of overlapping scales which protect the seeds that grow tucked between them. Cones can be smooth and egg-shaped as on cedar and fir trees, or long, woody and brown as on pine and spruce trees. Another distinctive thing about most conifer trees is their tough needle-like leaves.

What are conifer woodlands like?

Most conifer trees are evergreens. This means they shed and replace a few leaves at a time all year round, so they always look green. **Deciduous** trees shed all their leaves at once in autumn. Most conifer trees also grow tall and straight and do not spread their branches wide like many **broadleaved** trees. This means they can grow closely together and form dense stands of trees. With less space between the trees and branches covered in tightly packed leaves all year round, conifer woodland is much darker than broadleaved woodland.

There may be different kinds of conifer growing side-by-side, such as pine, spruce and fir, in coniferous woodland. Most have needle-like leaves, thick bark and grow their seeds in cones. ↓

On the forest floor

Conifer leaves take much longer to rot down and return their **nutrients** to the soil. This means the **leaf litter** on the floor of conifer woodland is less **fertile** and more **acidic** than that in most broadleaved woodland. As a result, fewer kinds of small plants grow there. Bracken is a type of **fern** that grows new fronds (leaves) from an underground stem. Pincushion moss grows in small mounds on damp soil or on rotting logs. A few flowering shrubs, such as heather and bilberry, flourish in sunny patches. Toadstools and other **fungi** grow among the leaf litter.

↑ The tough, leathery leaves of conifers survive and make food even in cold temperatures.

When you wander through woodland be careful never to touch any fungi, such as toadstools. The name toadstool means 'seat of death' – most are very poisonous to eat and touch. Fly agaric is a poisonous toadstool, often found in pine woods, that can grow to 16 centimetres high and 25 centimetres across. It has a bright red top with white spots that warns hungry animals to leave it alone.

Coniferous wildlife

Conifer woodlands can appear to be dark and quiet places but there is plenty of activity going on in them. They are homes to many different animals who are specially **adapted** to live here.

Insects

Tiny **insects** called soil mites live among the soil and feed on **fungi** in the **leaf litter**. The female pine sawfly cuts open pine needles lengthways and lays her eggs inside them. The **larvae** that hatch look like little green caterpillars. They eat vast quantities of needles. Wood ants live in large groups called colonies and make nests beneath mounds of pine needles. They roam over the woodland floor looking for caterpillars and other insects to take back to the nest to eat.

Wood ant colonies build nests from huge mounds of pine needles. Beneath the pine needles are complex networks of underground tunnels in which the wood ants live and **breed**. ↓

Birds

Many birds are small enough to fly through dense conifer woodland. The siskin is a small, lively finch that eats mainly seeds. Goldcrests have a golden-yellow head stripe and firecrests have a flash of fiery orange. At around 9 centimetres long, these are the smallest birds in the British Isles. They live amongst pine, spruce and fir trees, hunting for insects and spiders.

Some **birds of prey** hunt amongst conifers. Sparrowhawks and larger goshawks fly fast, twisting and turning between trees in pursuit of their **prey**. They grab small **mammals** and other birds using long sharp claws.

Mammals

A pine marten has a long, slender body, chestnut fur, a bushy tail for balance and sharp claws on its feet. It climbs trees and leaps nimbly between conifer branches and eats mice, squirrels, birds, insects and fruit. Red deer are the largest kind of deer in the British Isles. They live mainly in the Highlands of Scotland but also in parts of England. Red deer eat a range of food from bark, young shoots and **buds** of conifer trees to grasses and heather.

Red squirrel

If you walk through pine or spruce woodland and see chewed **cones** it may be a sign that squirrels live there. Squirrels hold the hard cones in their front paws and chew to get the seeds inside. Red squirrels are **native** to conifer forests in northern England and Scotland. They get their name from their red fur. Squirrels make nests called dreys out of twigs and moss in the forks of trees to have their young in.

The Black Wood of Rannoch in Perthshire is one of the largest areas of **native** Scots pine woodland left in Scotland. It is a remaining part of the Caledonian Forest, which once covered much of the Highlands.

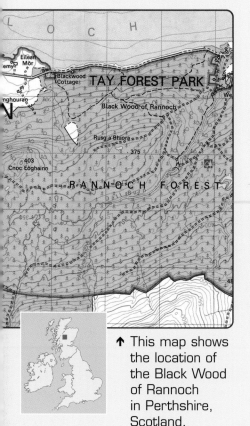

↑ This map shows the location of the Black Wood of Rannoch in Perthshire, Scotland.

Scots pines have wide-spreading branches and twisted blue-green needles. They lose their lower branches as they grow tall. This provides space for a rich layer of plant life to establish itself underneath, including heather, bilberry and juniper. **Broadleaved** trees such as birch and rowan also thrive on the **acidic** soil here.

Insect life

The rich **insect** life of Black Wood includes Scottish wood ants – which are hairier than those in England – wood wasps, sawflies and dragonflies. Rannoch looper moths live only in pine woodlands in this area. Their **larvae** feed on bilberry plants.

Wood wasp larvae live inside old pine logs and eat wood. The female ichneumon wasp uses her long, sharp egg-laying tube to bore into the logs and lay eggs on a wood wasp larva. The ichneumon larvae that hatch burrow into the wood wasp larvae and eat them from the inside!

↑ Some Scots pines in Black Wood are hundreds of years old. The bark peels off the top of old Scots pine trunks to show the orange-red wood beneath.

Birds of the Black Wood

The birds of the Black Wood include two Scottish **species** – capercaillies and Scottish crossbills. Capercaillies are large birds, about 50 centimetres tall, with black and dark green feathers and a red flash above the eyes. They live mainly on the ground and only fly short distances. In Black Wood young capercaillie eat wood ants and the adults eat berries and leaves from bilberry and heather plants. Older birds eat **buds** and twigs from young pine trees and large quantities of pine needles. Capercaillies have special strong stomachs to break down their tough foods. Pine martens sometimes eat capercaillie chicks and eggs they find between the pine trees.

Other animals in the Black Wood

Other animals that live in the Black Wood include red squirrel, pine martens, adders and deer. The red and roe deer that live in the Black Wood are a problem. They graze especially heavily on pine, birch and rowan seedlings. This means that new **native** trees struggle to establish naturally as older trees die.

↑ The Scottish crossbill gets its name from its unusual beak, which has hooked ends that cross over each other. This makes it an ideal tool for twisting apart the scales of pine cones to get at the seeds deep inside.

19

Mixed woodland

Mixed woodland contains a mix of **coniferous** and **broadleaved** trees. It is woodland where no single tree **species** covers more than three-quarters of the ground.

Mixed woodlands in the British Isles usually contain different smaller areas each dominated by one species. For example, an area of mostly beech trees may be next to a patch of hazel trees with a conifer **plantation** nearby. In other woodlands broadleaved trees grow amongst the conifers. What grows where is partly due to the soil. For example, birch trees grow well on dry, low-**nutrient** soils, ash grows well on chalky soil and alder and cherry grow well in damp soil.

Life on a dead tree

When woodland trees die, many different organisms gradually break them down and help to release their nutrients back into the soil. New plants use the nutrients in the soil to grow. Creatures such as millipedes and slugs eat dead leaves, releasing some of their goodness into the soil after they pass through the animals' bodies. As bark falls off a dead tree, **insects** and other animals eat away at the wood inside. When the trunk is weakened it is easily blown over by the wind. **Fungi** get to work on the fallen trunk or the remaining stump, gradually turning it into a soggy pulp.

Mixed wildlife

Mixed woodland contains a mix of many of the animals that live in broadleaved and coniferous woodland. Some tend to stay in one area. For example, red squirrels prefer to live among the conifer trees. Others may move between the different kinds of trees. One of the reasons for the population increase of grey squirrels is because they are able to feed and live among both kinds of trees. As in other kinds of woodland, many of the animals are **nocturnal**, so you are unlikely to see them on a daytime woodland walk.

Tawny owls

Tawny owls are the birds you might hear calling in woodland in the dead of night. 'Twit-twoo', 'hoo-woo-hoo' and 'ke-wick' are the more common sounds they use to communicate with each other. Tawny owls sit in woodland trees at night and listen out for **prey** on the ground. They hunt small birds, **mammals**, frogs and insects by swooping down onto them. Owls swallow prey whole and cough up parts they cannot digest, such as bones and teeth, in parcels called pellets. You may find owl pellets on the woodland floor.

Forest of Dean, England

The Forest of Dean in Gloucestershire and Herefordshire is the largest area of mixed woodland in Britain. It contains areas of mixed **broadleaved** trees including oak, lime, ash, birch and sweet chestnut. There are also large **plantations** of **conifers** such as spruce and larch. A great variety of wildlife lives here, such as foxes, badgers, dormice and fallow deer, as well as butterflies and birds.

↑ This map shows the location of the Forest of Dean in Gloucestershire and Herefordshire. There are several towns and many villages in the forest.

Woodland butterflies

The Forest of Dean is home to over 30 different **species** of butterfly. Holly blue butterflies group around holly bushes at the edges of clearings. They lay their eggs on young holly leaves that their **larvae** feed on.

Adult speckled wood butterflies feed on droplets of **honeydew** produced by aphids feeding on leaves. Males often rest in patches of sunlight so females that are ready to **breed** can see them. If another male flies into their sunny patch, they fly in spirals around it to chase it away.

↑ Small pearl-bordered fritillaries, like this one, usually feed on the nectar of violet, bramble or thistle flowers that grow in woodland clearings.

Bird life

One of the things that makes the Forest of Dean so special for wildlife is that such a variety of birds is found there. In the broadleaved woodlands, nuthatches, treecreepers, jays and green woodpeckers may be seen. The green woodpecker often searches clearings for ants, which it eats using a sticky tongue up to 20 centimetres long! Among the conifers, crossbills, siskins and flocks of coal and long-tailed tits forage for seeds. Nightjars are brown mottled birds that lie on the ground or on dead branches during the day. At dusk they fly with mouths open, hunting insect **prey** such as moths.

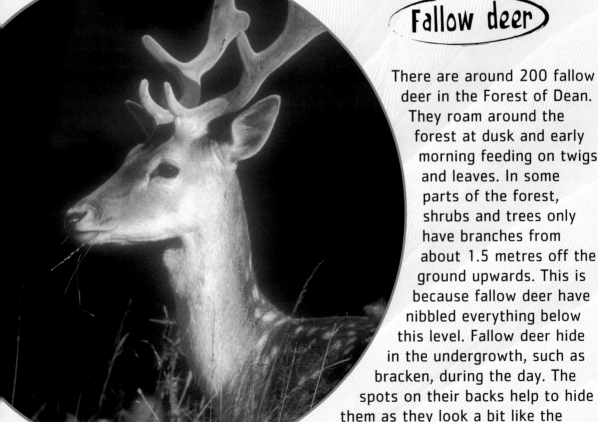

Fallow deer

There are around 200 fallow deer in the Forest of Dean. They roam around the forest at dusk and early morning feeding on twigs and leaves. In some parts of the forest, shrubs and trees only have branches from about 1.5 metres off the ground upwards. This is because fallow deer have nibbled everything below this level. Fallow deer hide in the undergrowth, such as bracken, during the day. The spots on their backs help to hide them as they look a bit like the natural patches of light under leafy trees.

Seasons in woodlands

As winter changes to spring and then summer, the weather gets warmer and the days get longer – there are more hours of light. Sunlight is the main source of **energy** for plants and it triggers plants to grow and produce flowers. Plants are the basis for all **food webs**, and as plant activity increases, so does animal life.

Spring and summer

In spring, before branches above fill with leaves and block out much of the light, the floor of **broadleaved** woodland is full of flowers. The **buds** on the trees begin to swell, and then burst into leaf. **Insects** hatch from eggs or emerge from **hibernation** to feed on the new plants. Bird song fills the woods as male birds sing from the trees to attract females who will lay eggs and have young at this time of plenty. Most woodland animals, such as badgers and squirrels, have their young in spring or summer. There is plenty of food about so young animals can grow big and strong enough to survive the cold of winter when it comes.

Many woodland flowers, such as bluebells and wood anemones, spend winter as bulbs underground. They burst into life as the days get warmer and lighter. ↓

Winter woodlands

In broadleaved woodlands leaves fall from the trees in winter. The trees stop growing through winter and rest until spring, living on stored energy. Flowering plants store energy in underground **bulbs** or roots. The lack of leaves makes it harder for animals to hide from **predators** and means that **herbivores** have little to eat.

Most adult insects die but leave eggs or **larvae** buried in soil or hidden in cracks in the tree bark, ready to emerge the following spring. Insect-eating woodland birds, such as warblers, **migrate** to warmer countries where they will be able to find food. Squirrels and many other small woodland animals spend most of the winter sleeping in warm hidden nests. Some woodland animals store food for winter. In autumn squirrels and jays collect nuts and bury them in the woodland floor to return to when food is scarce.

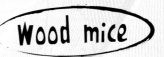

Wood mice

Wood mice live in woodlands all year round. They survive by changing their diet with the seasons. In spring they eat buds. In summer they eat caterpillars, worms and centipedes. In autumn they eat blackberries and **fungi**, like that below. In winter they eat acorns and seeds.

← In autumn, leaves of **deciduous** trees change colour and start to fall from branches.

Woodlands under threat

Between the 1900s and 1980s many thousands of square kilometres of ancient woodland in the British Isles were chopped down. Much of the cleared land was replanted with fast-growing **conifer plantations**. These could be more rapidly harvested and sold for timber than slower-growing **native** trees. Other cleared land was used for building houses, factories and schools for the growing British population or for farmland. Although native woodland is not being cut down as fast today, it is still threatened by people who want to create new airports, rubbish dumps and other developments.

Get this!

Only about 2 per cent of the British Isles is covered with ancient woodland.

Fewer species

The plants and animals that live in woodlands are dependent upon each other. Native trees, especially **broadleaved** kinds, are at the heart of **food webs** involving many more **species** than **introduced** trees. For example, native woodland trees such as oak are home to around 300 different **insect** species, while introduced species such as sycamore only have around 15! Fewer insect species attract a smaller range of **predators** such as birds.

Some woodland **habitats** in the British Isles are still being cut down to clear land for people to use. This broadleaved woodland is in north Wales. →

The increased amount of conifer plantations has reduced the variety of plants and animals in the British Isles. What is more, some introduced species are invading native woodland. For example, sycamore seeds that blow into woodlands grow very quickly. They take up space and light and make it difficult for young native trees to establish themselves.

Natural causes

Sometimes woodlands are damaged by natural events. In heavy storms in 1987 and 1990 around nineteen million trees were blown down in the British Isles. A future threat may be **climate change**. Scientists believe that the weather is becoming hotter and drier. If this happens, more insect pests may come to Britain from other countries and damage or threaten treasured woodland plants such as bluebells.

↑ When people illegally dump rubbish in woodland, the waste not only looks bad it can also harm or trap animals.

English elm

The elm is an example of a native tree that was once widespread in England. However, since the 1960s, up to 30 million elm trees have been killed by Dutch elm disease. This is a disease caused by **fungus**. The fungus is carried and passed on to elm trees by beetles that feed on their bark. Once a tree is infected, the disease spreads rapidly to other trees around it.

Protecting woodlands

Woodlands need to be protected. They are beautiful places where we can relax and see fascinating plants and animals. Woodlands are vital **habitats** for the wide range of plants and creatures that live there. Trees supply wood and other useful products. They are also essential producers of the **oxygen** that living things, including people, need to live.

Get this!

In recent years woodland cover has increased in the British Isles by about 100 square kilometres each year.

Changing woodlands

Since the 1980s, there has been a change in attitude to forest and woodland planting. Instead of planting just **conifers**, the Forestry Commission now encourages woodland owners to plant more mixed woodlands. Mixed woodlands usually supply a wider range of homes for living things and more wood products than conifer **plantations**.

Conservation organizations

Some ancient woodlands are still under threat. **Conservation** organizations are groups of people who work to protect wildlife and their habitats. The Woodland Trust raises money to buy ancient woodlands that are in danger of being destroyed. The Woodland Trust also puts pressure on the government to protect the remaining ancient woodland areas.

The Woodland Trust has helped save about 1000 woodlands from destruction with the help of local protestors. →

Woodland management

People look after woodlands to keep the trees healthy and to make sure new seedlings are able to grow. One way they do this is by thinning trees out – cutting down weak, spindly trees to provide room for healthier trees to spread out. Thinning also creates a mixture of light and shade in woodland. This encourages the growth of smaller plants, such as wildflowers, that attract wildlife.

Cutting down unwanted trees

People sometimes cut down unwanted trees – for example, sycamore – in **native** woodland as they might spread and take over from the native **species**. They also cut down trees that are old or dead and could easily blow over in high winds and injure people. Woodland managers use some cut trees for wood but leave others to decompose (rot away) on the woodland floor. This returns **nutrients** to the soil, helping new tree seedlings and other plants grow. Old trees also provide shelter and food for wildlife.

Hazel trees

People sometimes create open woodland spaces by cutting quick-growing trees such as hazel down to a stump. This is called coppicing. It encourages hazel trees to produce strong new shoots (branches) from their base.

← Many woodlands suffer when livestock, such as sheep, cattle or deer, eat all the **buds** and new growth on seedlings, which stops them growing into new trees. Plastic tubes help protect young trees from animal damage.

Glossary

acid/acidic acidic soils hold on to nutrients, so there are few available for plants to use

adapted/adaptable when a living thing has special features that allow it to survive in its particular habitat

antennae pair of feelers on an insect's head used to feel or taste

bacteria microscopic organisms that are found in the soil, water and air

birds of prey birds that hunt animals for food

breed when a male and female animal have babies

broadleaved describes kinds of tree with broad, flat leaves

bud swelling on a plant stem containing tiny young overlapping leaves or petals

bulb underground bud protected by layers of thick fleshy leaves such as an onion

climate change change in weather patterns over many years

cone part of conifer tree made up of overlapping scales where seeds grow

conifer kind of tree that makes seeds in cones, usually with needle-like leaves

conservation taking action to protect plants, animals and wild habitats

deciduous kind of plant that loses all its leaves before winter

energy all living things need energy in order to live and grow

evaporation when water turns from a liquid to a gas

fern type of plant such as bracken

fertile describes soil that is rich in nutrients

food web diagram that shows how food energy is passed from plants to animals

fungi plant-like living things such as mushrooms that do not make their food by photosynthesis

germinate when a new plant grows roots and shoots as it emerges from a seed

habitat place where plants and animals live

herbivore animal that eats plants

hibernation deep sleep during cold weather

honeydew sweet, sticky liquid that oozes from aphids as they eat plants

insect six-legged animals which, when adult, have three body sections: head, thorax (chest) and abdomen (stomach)

introduced when a plant or animal is brought to one country from another country

invertebrate animal without a backbone

larvae young stage in life cycle of some animals, between hatching from an egg and becoming an adult

leaf litter layer of rotting leaves on a woodland floor

lichen small, plant-like organism often found on bare rocks

mammals type of animal with some hair on their bodies. Female mammals can give birth to live young which they feed on milk from their bodies.

migrate when animals regularly move from one place to another

native living naturally in a particular place

nocturnal active at night

nutrients chemicals that nourish organisms

oxygen gas in the air all around us that living things need to live

photosynthesis how plants make their own food using water, carbon dioxide (a gas in the air) and energy from sunlight

plantation area of trees growing closely together that were planted by people

pollination when pollen travels from the male parts of one flower to the female parts of another flower to start a seed growing in the second flower

predator animal that catches and eats others

prey animal caught and eaten by another

species group of living things that are similar in many ways and can breed together

Find out more

Books

Bellamy's Changing World: The Forest, David Bellamy and Jill Dow (Simon & Schuster, 1991)

Biomes Atlases: Temperate Forests, John Woodward (Raintree, 2003)

Collins Gem: Trees, Alistair Fitter (Collins, 2002)

Taking Action: WWF, Louise Spilsbury (Heinemann Library, 2000)

Websites

The Forestry Commission has a website full of information about forests in the British Isles. The 'Wild Woods' section covers the wildlife and different types of woodland you may encounter: www.forestry.gov.uk/forestry/wildwoods

Groups that help look after British woodland include:
www.woodland-trust.org.uk (The Woodland Trust)
www.english-heritage.org.uk (English Heritage)
www.snh.org.uk (Scottish Natural Heritage)

The WWF (Worldwide Fund for Nature) is working to protect forests around the world from being cut down illegally. See: www.panda.org/forests4life

Index